LEADERSHIP

MONTY PYTHON AND THE HOLY GRAIL

BY RICHARD D. PARKER, PH.D.

Book•nol•o•gy

n. delivering useable information and knowledge
that adds value to people's lives

A BUSINESS & EDUCATIONAL IMPRINT FROM ADDUCENT
www.AdducentInc.com

LEADERSHIP LESSONS FROM
MONTY PYTHON AND THE HOLY GRAIL

BY RICHARD D. PARKER, PH.D.

LEADERSHIP LESSONS FROM MONTY PYTHON AND THE HOLY GRAIL

Richard D. Parker, Ph.D.

Paperback ISBN: 9781937592752

Published by Booknology (a business and educational imprint from Adducent)

Jacksonville, Florida

www.AdducentInc.com

TABLE OF CONTENTS

DEDICATION

To Dr. Lynn Butler-Kisber of McGill University's Faculty of Education, who is a true champion of learning and leadership.

To Dr. J. Kenneth Robertson, former Director General of Champlain Regional College in Canada, a true leader in every sense of the word, and who taught me more about the subject of leadership than I could have ever imagined.

Introduction

There are thousands – if not tens of thousands or hundreds of thousands – of books and articles on leadership that one can easily pick up and read. This work is not designed to impart a specific theory of leadership or replace any other work on the subject. When I began my teaching career as a doctoral student at the University of Alabama in the fall of 1999, I had no idea where that path might lead me. What I did discover in those early days was that my students enjoyed how I used film clips to illustrate points from course material. Later, after I had earned my Ph.D. and moved on to fill tenure-track faculty positions at both public and private universities, I discovered that the use of film was beneficial in many disciplines.

By the time I began teaching graduate classes, I knew that I had some good material to work with, but the by far most radical idea I had was to incorporate scenes from *Monty Python and the Holy Grail* into the courses I taught on leadership communication. At the beginning of each semester, the students were baffled by the line of reasoning I followed in using this film to point out certain lessons in leadership. However, when I began linking the scenes in the film to materials we read in class, the connections started to take. And after a while, the students figured out why I was forcing them to watch these often-outlandish scenes from a 1970s-cult film.

I left the academic world in 2014 to pursue other activities, including completing this manuscript, but I still feel that the leadership lessons which are found in *Monty Python and the Holy Grail* are worth sharing with a broader audience. You don't necessarily have to have seen the film to read this book, but I suspect it might help. And you certainly don't have to read the associated academic literature that my students read to relate to the lessons I've identified from the film. Rather than presenting the material randomly, as I did when I was a professor, I've organized the topics in this book in the same order that events appear in the film. I believe that this will make the material easier to follow and more enjoyable to read.

As I stated earlier, this is not a piece of written work based on theory. I believe that the practical application of leadership lessons can directly benefit those who wish to become better leaders in the real world. I've referenced some of the materials that were used in my courses, a few of which do contain a decent theoretical background, but my intention was to deliver a book that the average person can read, enjoy and pass along if they wish. I truly hope you'll enjoy this book and perhaps take seriously some of the lessons that can be gleaned from one of the most epic comedies produced in the 20th century.

Richard D. Parker, Ph.D.
Somewhere South of Castle Aaarrghh
November 2017

Chapter One

The Lesson of Coconuts and Swallows

"You've got two empty halves of coconut and you're banging them together."
- Castle guard to King Arthur

The opening scene of *Monty Python and the Holy Grail* sets the stage for our medieval adventure, bringing King Arthur and his "trusty servant" Patsy to a castle in which Arthur wants to have a meeting with the lord who lives there. Upon his arrival, Arthur introduces himself with much grandeur as the reigning monarch of the land and makes what he believes are impressive claims. Unfortunately, the castle guards atop the ramparts are a bit confused, as Arthur has introduced Patsy as his "trusty servant." The guards are confused because they thought they heard a horse approaching the castle, but it was only the sound of Patsy, who's carrying a pack and banging two empty halves of a coconut together. This sounds remarkably like the hoofbeats of a horse. Because the encounter is so outlandish, the guards want to know more about the coconuts, and how someone claiming to be "King of the Britons, defeater of the Saxons, sovereign of all England" found them.

The encounter leads to an absurd question and answer session between Arthur and the guards, in which the guards refuse to remark on Arthur's declared reason for being there in the first place. During the discussion on how a coconut came to be in Britain, Arthur inadvertently mentions that swallows fly south for winter, and this sends the conversation veering so far off course that it becomes unrecoverable. Deciding not to waste any more time, Arthur and Patsy depart from the castle, leaving the guards behind to ponder the involvement of swallows in bringing a tropical fruit to a temperate zone. Thus, the meeting with the lord of the castle never takes place.

The castle guards really aren't at fault here. They've been presented with a situation they simply find perplexing. How can they accept that Patsy is a surrogate horse when he's simply a man banging two empty halves of coconut together? Obviously, it is a situation they would like to have resolved before they move along to something else, namely, inform their lord of Arthur's presence and deliver Arthur's request to meet with him.

While the castle guards are not at fault, they are actually a big part of the problem encountered in this lesson. King Arthur has made a simple request of the guards to go and tell the castle lord that he's there. But the guards' main objective, vis-a-vis their participation in this meeting, is to discover how an object as alien as a coconut has found its way onto their island rather than to do what Arthur ultimately wants them to do. Because Arthur has mentioned swallows in the context of answering their question about where he got the coconuts, the guards now wish to explore this point further to determine whether the reasoning is rational. So, rather than carrying out his request, the guards have managed not only to get off topic but have digressed so far from the point of the meeting that Arthur simply gives up and leaves without having accomplished his main objective.

This lesson may have been the example taken from *Monty Python and the Holy Grail* that I most frequently used while teaching graduate courses on leadership communication for several years. Business professionals will be quick to admit that one of the biggest pitfalls in any meeting is that of digression or getting off topic. How much time is wasted annually in meetings when one person notices something that has no relevance to the agenda and ends up diverting the entire course of the discussion?

In a 1998 Harvard Business School article entitled "The Pitfalls of Meetings and How to Avoid Them," author Edward Prewitt outlined a very good formula to improve the effectiveness of meetings and reduce the time spent in them. Because so many managers come to meetings disorganized or lacking vital elements, many employees often complain that meetings are a huge waste of time and, subsequently, are often not only unpopular but in many cases even "dreaded."

There are many reasons why meetings can frequently be problematic. People arrive late or leave early. Sometimes managers call for a meeting without creating an agenda. One staff member dominates conversations at meetings and fails to give others an opportunity to provide input. And those who are running the meetings may have poor time management skills, one of the most hated aspects of meetings. Independent time keepers, who are usually not the managers running the meetings, are often not assigned to keep the meeting within the scheduled timeframe. But the number one problem that has a greater impact than almost all others (and frequently can impact the problems discussed above) is digressing from the purpose of the meeting. Students who took my classes knew exactly what I meant when I referenced "coconuts and swallows" after having reviewed this lesson with them, and they could easily relate that experience back to those gained in their own companies and other organizations in which they took part. Think for a moment and then ask yourself: "Do I have castle guards who discuss 'coconuts and swallows' in my own organization?"

The Lesson of Coconuts and Swallows, which is critical to your success as a leader, is this: don't get sidetracked from your main goals by unimportant distractions in your meetings with others.

CHAPTER TWO

THE LESSON OF
THE UNDERTAKER

"Bring out your dead!"
- The Undertaker

Following the disastrously unproductive meeting between Arthur, Patsy and the castle guards, we next encounter the King in the scene where an unusual transaction is taking place. An undertaker is seen moving through a village, calling for those still living to bring out their dead. One villager appears with a body and is ready to pay the undertaker's nine pence per corpse disposal fee, but the villager appears to have jumped the gun so to speak.

9

While the undertaker is willing to remove those, who have passed on to join the "choir invisible," his main requirement is that they be truly dead before he takes them. After an argument ensues between the not-quite-dead old man and the relative trying to get rid of him, and the latter does a bit of negotiating with the undertaker, an arrangement is made, a crucial blow is given, and the body is loaded on the cart. While this is not a lengthy scene in the film, it does provide an important lesson that leaders can readily appreciate.

From the settings of the scene, we know that the village through which the undertaker is traveling is not a very pleasant place to live. But in true Monty Python spirit, the writers have found a way to inject a bit of humor into the bleakest of circumstances. The villager is all too eager to rid himself of an old man for whom he no longer wishes to provide. On a humanitarian level, the scene is absolutely appalling, but let's set that aside for the moment and look at what's really happening. Even though the old man is still alive and actively protests being turned over to the undertaker, the villager insists that he doesn't have very long to live anyway. Even when the old man tries to demonstrate that he can still do things like go for a walk, the villager ignores his efforts and retorts "you're not fooling anyone." The undertaker must knock the old man over the head before the villager can unload his burden and carry on with his life.

So, what's the lesson here? Well, quite simply, it's to take care and try not to deliver something before it is ready to go. We all have tasks that we enjoy and those that we'd rather not do. Leaders are expected to set examples for others. They demonstrate what is acceptable and set expectations. While writing this book, I've had to write and edit and re-write and edit again to whip it into a publishable shape. If I were to deliver a half-finished product to a publisher, no one would knock the book on its proverbial head to finish it off. I simply wouldn't get very far in sending out an unfinished manuscript to a publisher. On many occasions, students tried to deliver an assignment to me that was only partially completed. Even if, like the undertaker, I had done them a "favor" by accepting it in an incomplete state, they assuredly would not have liked the outcome. My best strategy to deal with these situations was to tell them that the best way to avoid disappointment was to make sure that the work was complete before it was delivered.

Imagine for a minute that you are the CEO of a major US airline. Let's say that you have placed a large order with Boeing for their newest and most fuel-efficient airliners. What would your opinion of Boeing be, if your new airplanes were delivered with no seats, no cabin lighting, or only one engine? Could you reasonably be expected to provide a service (not just good, friendly, or quality service but basic service –

such as getting from point A to point B) for your passengers? What kind of situation would you put your employees in, if they had to explain these deficiencies to passengers who were trying to take a trip somewhere? And what would people think about your airline?

Now, let's look at this from the other perspective. Let's say that you are the project manager for Boeing and have sent out airplanes to major customers before those airplanes were finished being built. What kind of explanations are you going to give about why the planes were delivered before they were finished? What other responsibilities have you failed to fulfill? Is this the first time this type of thing has happened or has this been going on for a while? And – probably the most important question – how long can you expect to keep your job if this type of behavior continues? Delivering something before it is ready to its intended destination can be the cause of some major league problems for you, for the person expecting the delivery and even for the item that is being delivered. At the very least, it's highly inconvenient for all parties involved. And don't forget that, in this scene, it's the undertaker himself who has to finish off the old man. The villager asks the undertaker to hang around for a while and do him a favor. We know the undertaker has no time for this, after all, the Robinsons lost nine today. How many of us can get away with having the people to whom we're delivering things finish the job for us? I suspect that it's not many.

It's important for leaders to set an example and encourage those who are following them to hold high standards. But let's also remember the importance of meeting deadlines. In the business world, maintaining deadlines is critical. I once had a student who turned in a final report a day late, because he said he'd rather get a lower grade due to a deadline penalty than turn in something that was only half-finished. I might have accepted this argument had the assignment not been given six weeks earlier. The student's paper was first rate but, because he missed the deadline, he suffered a grade penalty. The student knew the cost of missing the deadline but handed in the assignment late anyway.

Although I argue that things shouldn't be delivered before they are ready, I also don't advocate the outright rejection of timelines or deadlines to deliver a better product. Leaders know that procrastination is the enemy of efficiency and good service. Nothing should be delivered before it is ready, but you can't wait forever to deliver something good. If you do, your competition will get the better of you on nearly all occasions. Consider for a moment that you want to build a swimming pool in your backyard and invite your neighbors over for a party. Let's say that you state, "I'm going to do that," and start digging a hole but stop short of filling it in with cement and procrastinate even further in that you put off buying a filtration system. Now, let's say the hole has been there for six weeks and you've done no additional work; meanwhile, your next-door neighbor has not only started digging a hole but has also rented a cement mixer and ordered a diving board and a slide. How will you feel in another four weeks when you still have a big, gaping hole in your backyard, and all the neighbors you wanted to invite over for a fun afternoon are next door enjoying your neighbor's new pool and a barbeque? You wouldn't invite them to come over to swim in a simple hole in your backyard, would you?

If you need more help understanding this lesson, consider the old advertising slogan for Paul Masson Wines: "We will sell no wine before its time." Would the world-famous Bordeaux wineries Chateau Lafite-Rothschild or Chateau Latour have produced some of the best-rated wines if they had immediately sent their products to market before they had let them age for the appropriate amount of time in oak barrels? Well, for upwards of $400 a bottle, I certainly hope not!

The lesson of the undertaker is an important one: Don't deliver something before it is ready.

CHAPTER THREE

THE LESSON OF
DENNIS THE PEASANT

"Listen, strange women lying in ponds distributing swords is no basis for a system of government. Supreme executive power derives from a mandate from the masses, not from some farcical aquatic ceremony. I mean, you can't go around wielding supreme executive power just because some watery tart threw a sword at you."
- Dennis the Peasant

My favorite scene in *Monty Python and the Holy Grail* has always been King Arthur's encounter with Dennis the Peasant. When I had thoughts of becoming a political science professor, long before I decided to switch disciplines, I had tried to imagine how I could incorporate Dennis's discussion about the nature of "supreme executive authority" into the future lectures I would give on the nature of politics and political situations. Little did I realize at the time that the entire scene with Dennis and King Arthur represented a better metaphor for leadership and that the lessons I learned from their interactions would be the genesis of something bigger than merely showing the film clip in class for discussion.

The second significant interaction between King Arthur and others in the film takes place when Arthur encounters a group of peasants who have no lord but do seem to have an interesting sense of political theory and government. Arthur is uninterested in the peasants' system of government, as he doesn't recognize it as legitimate. He quickly becomes annoyed with a peasant named Dennis who does his best to set the King straight on how things ought to be in the world, especially when it comes to making "progress." The contempt is two-sided, as Dennis refuses to accept the legitimacy of Arthur's crown and the two finally become involved in a physical altercation when Dennis calls attention to the scene and Arthur calls Dennis a "bloody peasant" before storming away in utter frustration.

So, what's the lesson here? Well there are really two lessons to be learned: 1) not everyone will accept your authority as a leader, and 2) how you react and respond to those people will be noticed and noted by others.

Dennis doesn't accept Arthur's legitimacy as king of the realm. History is full of examples of people who do not accept those in positions of authority. Usually, those people never get a chance to interact with their leaders the way Dennis does with King Arthur. But rebels exist in the business world as well as in other settings, and they will challenge the leader's authority because they have more direct opportunities. There is an abundance of literature that discusses ways to deal with difficult people. Still, there isn't a "one size fits all" approach that has been universally accepted. All kinds of tests and categories can be used to define people based upon their education, social status, communication style, or any number of psychological variables, but understanding your own leadership style will help you decide how you might choose to deal with a rebel like Dennis, should you find yourself in King Arthur's shoes. How you choose to identify your own leadership style is not the topic of this book. What we are doing here is reviewing a series of lessons from one of the great cult classics of twentieth-century cinema. So, yes, rebels out there will refuse to accept authority and conform no matter what efforts (carrots or sticks) are invested. I'm sure that you can easily remember at least one Dennis the Peasant that you have met during your life, even if you must go all the way back to grade school. What may be more important, however, is the second lesson from this scene.

Arthur has a problem. Dennis is wasting his time explaining a system of government that Arthur doesn't recognize as legitimate. He's the ruler and has no time to spend talking to people who aren't quick to recognize that fact. So, having had enough of Dennis's lecture, he decides to step forward and take action. As Arthur shakes Dennis and repeatedly screams at him to shut up, wildly frustrated by Dennis's refusal to cooperate, onlookers gather to see what all the commotion is about. Dennis's screams of "Help! Help! I'm being repressed" have only served to gather the attention of others to what is happening. Ultimately, Arthur, quite obviously at his wit's end, calls Dennis a "bloody peasant" and stalks angrily away. Arthur's actions and reactions are being judged by those who are watching. He has just lost any chance he might have had to possibly get what he wanted from others on the scene.

How many times in our own lives have we done something like Arthur? I'm not talking about violence, of course, but how many times has our frustration gotten the better of us when we were dealing with someone who is being "impossible?" How many times have actions like Arthur's brought us success? Probably not very often. Usually, the result is loss: loss of time, effort, productivity and even potentially the respect of others around us. And, ultimately (and in my opinion, most importantly), loss of credibility as a leader.

In his book *It's Your Ship: Management Techniques from the Best Damn Ship in the Navy*, Captain Michael Abrashoff revisited the change of command ceremony that happened aboard *USS Benfold* as he took over as commanding officer. Captain Abrashoff explained how some of the crew members of *USS Benfold* gave the departing captain a less than respectful sendoff. At that moment, Abrashoff began to consider how he wanted his crew to remember him. Abrashoff's story is a remarkable one that has been told many times and appeared in many leadership textbooks.

While Abrashoff's lessons are very good, I would like to think that he might appreciate the story of Arthur's encounter with Dennis the Peasant based on his own experiences. He knew that his crew would carefully be watching his actions and reactions. He also knew that the crew had previously formed opinions and attitudes about management based on their experiences with the former captain. Abrashoff was determined to prove that he was a different type of captain, and he did so with astounding results. *USS Benfold* progressed from being a ship with a record of low retention and advancement among its crew members to the winner of the coveted Spokane Trophy, one of the US Pacific Fleet's most important awards.

Abrashoff describes some valuable lessons that the manager of any organization can appreciate and utilize. However, rather than provide a synopsis of Abrashoff's work, I would like to point out a harsh truth of reality: leaders are watched. Mike Abrashoff knew this truth, and King Arthur would have done well to have remembered it. The lessons we learn from the scene with Dennis the Peasant are important because leaders must always realize and understand that they will never be universally loved (even Presidents Roosevelt, Kennedy, Reagan and Clinton had their critics), and that how they respond to those who do not support them will be watched critically – and more importantly, remembered – by others.

The Lesson of Dennis the Peasant is twofold: 1) Not everyone will accept your authority as a leader, and 2) how you react and respond to those people will be noticed and noted by others.

Chapter Four

The Lesson of
the Black Knight

*"The Black Knight **always** triumphs!"*
- The Black Knight

In the scene that follows King Arthur's encounter with Dennis the Peasant, we see Arthur and Patsy traveling through a dark forest when, suddenly, they happen upon two knights who are locked in fierce combat. One of these is the infamous Black Knight. Arthur and Patsy quietly watch the battle as it progresses. Ultimately, the Black Knight prevails by slaying his opponent. Arthur, impressed by this knight's fighting skills, decides that he is worthy to join his knights at Camelot. Arthur approaches the knight, introduces himself and then invites the Black Knight to join him. Much to Arthur's disappointment, the knight appears to be disinterested and refuses to answer any of Arthur's questions. In fact, he doesn't speak at all, at least until Arthur decides to continue his journey.

When Arthur and Patsy attempt to cross the bridge which the Black Knight has been guarding, the Black Knight finally speaks, declaring that "none shall pass!" Arthur attempts to reason with the knight, but for naught. After refusing Arthur and Patsy passage across the bridge, the Black Knight engages in single combat with the King with disastrous consequences. The Black Knight loses limb after limb during the fight, but taunts Arthur, only increasing the King's ire and increasing the peril of his own situation as the scene unfolds. In the end, he can do nothing to prevent Arthur from crossing the bridge, and we last see him – a mere stump - in the worst possible circumstances.

The Black Knight would have done well to have read the legendary text written by Sun Tzu called *The Art of War*. Sun Tzu wrote more about the strategy of winning than the tactics of combat, and there are many parallels between business and war. Both are highly competitive enterprises in which people seek to achieve goals. In war, the ultimate goal is victory. In business, the ultimate goal happens to be profit. But like victory in war, profits can often be attained through a variety of ways, some of which are noble and some of which are nefarious.

Sun Tzu counsels his readers in *The Art of War* to win without fighting. He suggests that one must know one's self to achieve victory and that one must understand the circumstances, situations, and context before deciding to pick a fight with someone. Most importantly, Sun Tzu advises you not to fight unless you are sure of winning. Unless you have solid information or intelligence, you are likely to fail. And situations, where this type of knowledge is useful, are not necessarily limited to war or business.

The lesson of the Black Knight is a simple one: know when to quit. Despite the Black Knight's obvious skill in hand-to-hand combat, he is quickly dispatched by Arthur. Instead of yielding once Arthur has gained the advantage by cutting off his arm, the Black Knight continues to fight. What's worse is that the Black Knight refuses to accept that he is losing. Like the ostrich who buries his head in the sand to avoid something unpleasant, he ignores the obvious danger that he has placed himself in due to his continued aggression. Instead of doing what is necessary to preserve his own survival and let Arthur continue his journey, the Black Knight resorts to making excuses and denials about what's happened to him and continues to fight. How many times have we said to ourselves, "Tis but a scratch!" or "I've had worse" when we're really coping with a catastrophic situation?

If the Black Knight had only recognized that he had just suffered a major loss when Arthur cut off his arm and accepted that fact, he might not have ended up as a limbless torso left in the middle of a forest with no way to survive. Leaders often fail to recognize what can be learned from both Sun Tzu and the Black Knight. Sometimes you must know when to walk away from a situation or quit while you are ahead. The Black Knight's problem is that he's obsessed with preventing anyone from crossing over his footbridge. He continues to taunt and antagonize Arthur even after losing both arms. Even after Arthur cuts off a leg, he continues to be a nuisance. Finally, after having both legs cut off, he wants to "call it a draw," refusing to admit defeat. Then, after Arthur crosses the bridge, he accuses Arthur of "running away" and screams threats to bite his legs off.

In Gerald Michaelson's translation of *The Art of War,* featured in his book *Sun Tzu for Success,* Sun Tzu discusses the "five dangerous faults" of leadership. He writes:

1. If reckless, he can be killed.
2. If cowardly, he can be captured.
3. If quick-tempered, he can be provoked to rage and make a fool of himself.
4. If he has too delicate a sense of honor, he is liable to fall into a trap because of an insult.

5. If he is of a compassionate nature, he may get bothered and upset.

We know that the Black Knight, while a victorious combatant (prior to Arthur's arrival), is reckless and seems to have a delicate sense of honor given his reaction to Arthur's declaration that he is a "loony," but, ultimately, the Black Knight is a failure when he didn't need to be.

Leaders who live in denial, refusing to accept their losses and not knowing when to quit, may very easily end up just like the Black Knight. No arms, no legs and a distorted sense of reality that won't bring victory, profit, or success. There is something good to be said about being persistent. Many people have been successful solely on the basis that they refused to give up, but the vast majority of those people were not dealt the catastrophic blows the Black Knight received from Arthur. Still, being persistent for the sake of mere persistence is idiotic at worst and foolhardy at best. Tilting at windmills is a romantic gesture best left to Don Quixote and the other classic heroes and heroines in literature.

The Lesson of the Black Knight is simple: know when to quit.

CHAPTER FIVE

THE LESSON OF
THE WITCH'S TRIAL

"How do you know she is a witch?"
- Sir Bedevere

The first knight to join King Arthur in *Monty Python and the Holy Grail* is Sir Bedevere. We are first introduced to him as he tries to see if a bird can fly away with a coconut attached to a string that has been tied to its leg. As he is conducting this experiment, a mob comes to him with a woman they have accused of being a witch. They are seeking his permission to burn her, but he wants to know why they think she is a witch. After listening to their reasons, which make no sense at all to him, he convinces them that, if she weighs as much as a duck, it means she is a witch and, hence, they can burn her. Arthur witnesses this entire spectacle, since he introduces the element of the duck into the scene. Following the mob's departure with the woman – presumably to carry out the burning – Bedevere speaks with Arthur and asks him how he has so much knowledge. Once Arthur announces he is the King, Bedevere declares "my liege!" and kneels. Arthur now has been joined by his first knight, but has he acted too hastily in accepting Bedevere?

The lessons learned from this scene are especially important because many people suggest that more people need to develop and use their critical thinking skills in today's world. Sir Bedevere attempts to get the mob to consider whether they are truly correct in their accusation, asking them a series of questions designed to logically determine the truth of the woman's status as a witch. The only problem is that the entire line of reasoning Bedevere takes while asking the questions is completely faulty (not Fawlty, for those of you who were thinking it!).

Critical reasoning and thinking skills are often lacking in today's world because too many people think like members of a mob instead of like rational individuals. The villagers have decided to follow the mob for the thrill of seeing the woman burned as a witch, even though the direct evidence suggests she is not. Some would argue that perception is reality, but if one thinks critically, this argument must be put aside, and some serious questions asked. This is actually where Sir Bedevere gets it right. Rather than simply accepting the word of the people seeking to burn the woman, he attempts to walk them through (what he feels is) a reasonable way to make that determination by asking them a series of questions and find the truth by answering those questions.

Unfortunately, while Sir Bedevere's strategy is right, his tactics are all wrong, because he is not asking the members of the mob the right questions. Critical thinking is not just about examining evidence and asking questions; it's about piecing evidence together and knowing the right questions to ask. During my career as a professor, I attempted to illustrate the proper use of critical thinking skills by showing the 1957 film *Twelve Angry Men* each year. If you haven't seen this movie, put it next on your list. I'd be very surprised if you didn't enjoy the film and, at the same time, understand precisely what I am talking about after watching. In this film, a young man is placed on trial for murder, and 11 jurors want to convict him immediately. There's only one man holding out: juror number eight, who is played by Henry Fonda. Number eight's use of reasoning and logic are the foundation of the film, and by asking the right questions and using proper logic and reasoning, this character infuses the film with strength. The film is still popular almost 60 years after its release.

However, knowing the right questions to ask is only half of the lesson to be taken from this scene. I know this is a *Monty Python* film, and things are not supposed to be logical. That's fine for the purposes of enjoying the film. However, we need to put that aside for a moment and consider what Sir Bedevere and King Arthur have led the mob to believe. If the woman weighs as much as a duck, they reason, then she is made of wood and, therefore, is a witch. At least, this is Bedevere's strategy for proving the mob's accusation. So, they take her to Bedevere's largest scales and discover that she **does** weigh as much as a duck. And, thus, the mob carries her away. The problem is that Bedevere's logic is faulty (cut it out John Cleese fans, we're not going in any direction toward Torquay). And even worse than Bedevere's faulty logic is the fact that he's a "yes man."

Upon learning Arthur's identity, Bedevere immediately kneels before the king, indicating his subservience and is rewarded on the spot with a knighthood. Arthur is obviously gratified that he has finally found someone in the film who respects his authority as the monarch. As the movie continues, we learn more and more about the absurd logic that Bedevere follows. And Arthur listens to this with disastrous results (as we will see later in the Trojan Rabbit incident). We also know from the encounter with Dennis the Peasant that Arthur doesn't like people who challenge his authority, and we assume that he would listen to someone who respects his authority as king without question. Here's where we have an issue: Those who refuse to listen to those who aren't blind followers run the risk of facing embarrassment and failure. There's yet another issue: The "yes men" who use faulty logic to persuade those in authority aren't always axed when they should be. Leaders sometimes forgive their followers who display blind loyalty too easily, rather than listening to proper logic and answers they don't like. This is especially true in difficult circumstances, as leaders may need to hear from those who are willing to point out flaws in decisions, systems, or logic. These individuals often have attributes that, in fact, maybe more valuable to leaders than those of the yes men, who express their absolute and unconditional love for the emperor's new clothes. As a leader, it's sometimes necessary to step back and ask yourself if the advice and counsel you receive are in step with what you want to hear. If so, is that necessarily a good thing for you and/or your organization? Leaders often need to hear from people who can keep them from making poor decisions that are based on faulty logic and reasoning.

Leaders should always keep in mind both lessons from the trial of the witch: 1) Know the right questions to ask and 2) beware of faulty logic.

Chapter Six

The Lesson of Camelot

"On second thought, let's not go to Camelot,
'tis a silly place."
- King Arthur

Soon after Bedevere joins Arthur, and other knights are introduced in the film, the group rides toward Camelot, bringing us to one of the most beloved scenes in the movie. This particular scene is beloved because it contains one of the few songs in the entire film. It is so popular that it has actually been recreated in stop-motion animation using Lego building blocks. As Arthur and the knights spot Camelot, Arthur tells them to ride forth to their new home. Before they do so, however, the scene setting then switches to the castle interior, and we see an epic song and dance performed by knights who are already there. The song concludes and, based on this scene, Arthur decides he and his knights should not go to Camelot after all, since "'tis a silly place." He proceeds to take his knights elsewhere. While this scene has provided much inspiration to countless audiences and various creative artists over the years, it also provides us with an important lesson that leaders would be wise to consider.

Think about the last time you went into a store or restaurant and had a bad customer service experience. Take a moment to think hard and reflect on the situation. Can you remember the exact circumstances? Can you remember how you felt during this experience? Can you remember where this happened or the exact name of the business? Now, think for a moment; what was the name of the person who was responsible for the bad customer service experience? I'm willing to bet that most of you will be able to remember almost everything about the bad customer service experience, except the name of the person in the business with whom you dealt. But I will concede that, if the person really annoyed you or made you angry, you might have made a point of remembering the exact name of the person.

Now, I want you to take a moment and think about the last person you spoke with who truly impressed you. What was it about this person that impressed you so much? Was it how he or she was dressed? Was it the person's manner of speech or personal behavior? Was it the fact that he or she clearly knew a great deal about the topic of discussion? Was this person confident? Were they organized? Did they actually follow up and follow through as promised?

Let's go back to school for a moment. Can you think of the five best courses you took? In my case as an undergraduate, these were two history courses, a human development course, a science course and a Navy ROTC class. Now, the ironic thing is that I was a political science major, but none of what I would consider the best classes I had were in political science. So, why do I consider those courses to be the best? My professors in political science were outstanding. They did a superb job, so why didn't they make the cut? Honestly, it was because of the people who taught my top five courses, who included the chairman of the history department at Alabama, a Hubble Space Telescope astronomer and a professional naval officer. Not only did they know their materials, they were passionate about them.

Now, let's take a moment to look at the opposite case. I won't ask which of the courses you had in school were the five worst, but ask yourself what the very worst was. Chances are you'll remember it immediately. For me, it was a principles of accounting class. Apart from the fact that I was completely disinterested in the topic, the instructor – while a very nice person – did a horrible job of presenting the material to us. Absenteeism in the course was absurdly high, and the test material rarely reflected what we were taught in class. Based on the in-class quizzes, it was obvious that the instructor wasn't really serious about the material she was supposed to be teaching. How many of you were quizzed in your principles of accounting courses on what day of the week it was or the name of your pet? "On second thought, let's not go to Camelot, 'tis a silly place" indeed.

Okay, so the point of all of this is quite simple: presentations matter. Of course, most of us want our presentations to be taken seriously. Whether we want to show a prospect a new product or demonstrate a new service, deliver a report to our boss about the last quarter's productivity numbers, interview for a new job we really want, or even serve a quartet of real estate agents lunch at a local Italian restaurant, most of us really want to put our best foot forward. We'd like to be seen, acknowledged and appreciated for what we've done. Whether we recognize it or not, we're actively engaged in making presentations all the time. Many are formal, but most are informal. And those informal presentations are the ones that are usually noticed the most often. So, of course, we want to be professional and command respect among our co-workers and peers. For this reason, we tend to care how well we perform our duties on the job. Not many people intend to be silly or treat their work in a manner that could be interpreted as flippant.

But what about those people who really do attempt to present things well, by trying to be entertaining and make others smile, but don't have a clue that they are failing miserably? How many of us have taken the time and effort to pull aside (in a professional and chivalrous way) those people who are not quite getting it and give them a little bit of coaching?

A good friend of mine at a Canadian university once had a student who had enrolled in her MBA course, which was heavily focused on writing but wasn't a very good writer. The student was enthusiastic about the material the class was studying but did not comprehend that writing at the graduate level and, especially writing for courses in an MBA program, was not the same as the writing at the undergraduate level. The student attempted to insert humor into a serious research paper, attempting to earn points by making the professor smile, but this only resulted in a request to re-write the assignment for a reduced grade. The student was shocked when told that statements attempting to be funny had no place in a serious report. Similarly, during individual and group presentations in the class, the student managed to annoy everyone else by being overly dramatic. The retrospective view was that this would have been better in an audition or a drama course. The one thing that really struck my friend was that, during the group presentation, the student could not be seen from where she (the professor) was sitting in the classroom, and this student sounded angry, based on the tone of voice and speaking volume. I'm sure that was not the student's intention, but even the effect was not realized until the professor delivered her feedback after the presentations had been finished.

So, presentations do matter. And it is important to keep in mind that tailoring presentations to the expectations of your target audience matters even more. Any advertising executive will tell you that if you don't know your target audience, you can't effectively reach it. Additionally, you also need to know how your target audience likes to consume its information. So, how well do you know your target audiences? Do you know what they expect in terms of formal versus informal delivery? Are you checking in walk-in guests during Spring Break at the Motel 6 in Daytona Beach or are you helping someone who's a member of the Fairmont President's Club check into a suite at The Queen Elizabeth in Montreal?

Of course, the basic functions that take place during the interaction don't differ that much, but imagine what would happen at a 5-star hotel if you didn't have a bellhop to help with the luggage or a concierge to tell a new visitor where's the best place to go for a steak and a glass of cabernet in the city?

Knowing your material is only half of the recipe. In many cases, how you deliver it separates those who are successful from those who sit and Monday morning quarterback what went wrong for the following three weeks. I used to show my students a film clip from *The Hunt for Red October* that illustrates this point very well. In one scene of the film, Jack Ryan (played by Alec Baldwin) has been called by Admiral Greer (James Earl Jones) to join a briefing with the White House National Security Advisor on short notice. Ryan arrives at the White House, is handed a stack of papers that detail Soviet naval deployments during the last 24 hours, and asks who is giving the briefing. He is speechless when Greer announces that he's giving the briefing. Greer's reason: nobody knows the materials better than Ryan. Because he is an expert, he should be able to give an impromptu presentation that is credible and will ultimately be accepted by the powers that be.

Unfortunately, very few of us are as good at presenting as Jack Ryan. We must memorize our presentation, rehearse it and be ready to take questions that we may or may not have all the answers to. Not enough people schedule enough the time to practice their presentations; just running through your presentation a couple times can help your confidence tremendously! And then many of us still have to contend with stage fright. But if you know your material, understand your audience and rehearse your presentation effectively, you might actually get King Arthur and his knights to pay you a visit instead of deciding to go elsewhere.

The Lesson of Camelot is often taken for granted: Presentations matter! If you know your material, understand your target audiences' expectations and are able to effectively present information, you can open the doors to access some good opportunities. Otherwise, your messages to those who matter will not be well received, and the King and his knights may go elsewhere.

Chapter Seven

The Lesson of
the Trojan Rabbit

"Look, if we built this large wooden badger..."
- Sir Bedevere

Shortly after Arthur and his knights are charged by God to find the Holy Grail, they come upon a castle that is inhabited by a group of French soldiers. Arthur tries to enlist the support of the castle lord but is rebuffed by the French guards on the wall. These soldiers are not interested in helping Arthur but, instead, take up an adversarial role that will not be the last one seen in the film. The scene begins with Arthur requesting shelter for the evening and offering the French guards a chance to join them in the quest to find the Grail if they help them. The French, however, are having no part of it, and taunt and insult Arthur's party before hurling animals at them to drive them away. After this embarrassing retreat, Sir Bedevere believes he has an idea that will solve their problems.

Admittedly, a lot happens in this scene. Arthur and his knights are seeking a place to rest after their long journey, the French deliberately deceive them by claiming they have the Holy Grail, insults fly, violence follows, animals are catapulted over the castle walls, and a couple of people are squashed. But the heart of this lesson emerges from Arthur and his knights' responses to their failed counterattack on the French.

Borrowing a page from the ancient Greeks, the English decide to build a large wooden animal – in this case, a rabbit – in an attempt to repeat the success of the Trojan Horse. Of course, in true Monty Python fashion, it all goes horribly wrong, and the plan backfires with the French having the last laugh. The idea was sound; build a large wooden rabbit, give it to the French as a gift, then wait for nightfall to attack. The problem was that Sir Bedevere failed to carefully think all the details of the plan through before the knights set about building the rabbit and leaving it on the doorstep of the French castle.

Another important issue here is that Bedevere failed to effectively communicate the plan of action completely was until it was too late to correct the error that had occurred. Someone dropped the ball. Had it been Bedevere's responsibility to divulge all the information about the plan or had it been Arthur's responsibility to completely understand Bedevere's plan in its entirety and, thus, avoid making a bad mistake? As business executives regularly cite poor communication skills as the number one problem in the corporate world today, perhaps those at the top should spend some time reflecting on their timing when it comes to seeking information from subordinates.

In the mid-1990s catalog retailer, J. Peterman was enjoying a tremendous amount of success, not only from the sales generated from circulation of its iconic catalogs but also from its exposure on NBC's highest rated show at the time – *Seinfeld*. J. Peterman's management decided to expand their catalog sales into the Japanese market without really testing whether a concept that had been so successful in the United States would work as well in Japan. Unfortunately, Japanese consumers were not eager to purchase clothes through the mail, and the venture had to be abandoned. In this case, the management would have been wise to have had someone at a lower level research the marketing strategy (to see if an American-style catalog sales model would potentially work in Japan) and report their findings to the executive team.

It's essential to have enough information to make a critical decision to achieve success, no matter what your goal happens to be. Failing to communicate all information regarding the execution of a course of action is not only costly in terms of lost time and effort, but also in terms of lost credibility and reputation. By communicating all critical points of information in a timely fashion, leaders stand a much better chance at succeeding. When delegating tasks related to research to people in the lower levels of an organization, it's the leader's responsibility to make sure that everyone understands that communication is vital to organizational success – and specifically reporting findings, options, opinions, and recommendations – otherwise, you may end up attempting to dodge that rabbit you just tried to give away.

There is another lesson to be learned from this scene. Once the knights realize that a mistake has been made (i.e., deploying the rabbit without anyone inside to carry out the plan), Sir Bevedere quickly suggests they go back and build another large wooden animal, this time a badger. This idea is quickly vetoed (non-verbally), as Arthur smacks Bevedere on the side of the head. Shortly after this, the French return the wooden rabbit to Arthur and the knights in what may be one of the worst examples of re-gifting.

Arthur recognizes that the French are unlikely to fall for the same trick twice. Not only that, but he also recognizes that repeating the same exercise would be a waste of valuable resources (including time).

Arthur's reaction to Bedevere's ridiculous suggestion, however, is not exactly out of the ordinary in many organizations. While most leaders are not likely to react physically to suggestions to repeat things that do not work, there are plenty of examples of nonverbal reactions that are just as harsh. Leaders need to remember that, even when subordinates make mistakes, they often want to do their best to correct these and attempt to remain in their good graces.

University of North Texas communication professor Dr. Kim Sydow Campbell has written extensively on how important it is for managers to be able to recognize in-groups and out-groups in their organizations. She also describes how important contributions from those groups are to the effectiveness (or ineffectiveness) of organizational dynamics. To build effective rapport with their subordinates, managers must identify members of their "in-group" and take care in their communications with those who are in the "out-group." A sarcastic remark or biting comment that is expressed in an attempt to be humorous may work with those in your "in-group," but the same remark made to a person in the "out-group" could get the manager into some real trouble.

One of the biggest problems managers face while dealing with their subordinates is that most are unaware of the impact of their communications. Most managers do not know that they are not master communicators and the very few who do realize this have invested time to work on improving their communication skills. One of the reasons that Captain Michael Abrashoff got such incredible results as commander of the *USS Benfold* was that he understood the power of communication and employed it effectively to both his advantage and to improve the organization as a whole.

Another lesson leaders and subordinates would be wise to take away from this scene is that, when an opportunity to do something over again presents itself, this should never be taken for granted. Mistakes are made in many situations and under many circumstances, and people are not always afforded the opportunity to try to correct these mistakes. Think of the kicker who misses the uprights during the last-second field goal attempt of a football game for a conference championship or the person who purchases a plane ticket for a vacation, accidentally gets the dates wrong and doesn't realize it until it is too late to change them without paying a penalty. What would those individuals give for a chance to try again?

Naval aviators are some of the most fortunate people on the planet. When a young pilot first learns to land a multi-million-dollar airplane on the deck of a moving aircraft carrier at sea, he or she must do so under some of the most dangerous and stressful conditions imaginable. When a pilot misses the arresting cables on the deck of a carrier and must fly around for another attempt, this is called a bolter. An aviator who has a bolter is often sent back out the next day to fly again to get the landing right. And he or she is usually the first pilot in the squadron launched off the carrier. In many respects, the flight instructors who send these young people back out are doing them a tremendous favor by giving them the opportunity to get it right before they completely fail out. While some people may think that placing a person back into a situation that they are having trouble with may not be the best idea, the objective here is to give people a chance to learn from the mistakes, restore their confidence and achieve the objective: to qualify good men and women to land airplanes on the deck of the mightiest warships on the sea.

Think carefully about mistakes that either you or others in an organization to which you belong may have made. If there had been better knowledge and communication about what really needed to be accomplished and this had been shared with the appropriate people, could this have prevented the failure? Also, when was the last time you really appreciated having the chance to correct something that didn't go as planned? Those are points that are truly important to consider if we are to be successful leaders.

The Lesson of the Trojan Rabbit is twofold: 1) Knowing what you really want to do before you act will give you a greater chance of success; 2) appreciate it when you get an opportunity for a do-over – in some instances, these come rarely.

Chapter Eight

The Lesson of Sir Galahad

"It's not the real Grail!?!?"
- Sir Galahad

Sir Galahad is another knight from whom we can learn a couple of things in *Monty Python and the Holy Grail*. Believe it or not, his tale is supremely frustrating on more than one level. It is certainly the most risqué part of the film (and, in recent releases including on the one available on iTunes, an additional bit of dialogue has been placed back into the film that was not included in the original theatrical release), and it certainly leaves many viewers (especially the male ones) with the same keen sense of sympathetic disappointment as Sir Galahad.

Wandering alone through a wooded land, Sir Galahad spots what he believes is the shining image of the Holy Grail hovering above a nearby castle. Approaching the castle, he gains entry only to discover that it is inhabited by "eight score" young women who are younger than the drinking age in the United States. The young woman who has admitted Sir Galahad to "Castle Anthrax" notices that he is wounded and ushers him off to see the "doctors," but Galahad insists that he must find the Grail. Leaving the doctors, he stumbles across a chamber filled with many young women, one of whom admits that they have a beacon that is "Grail-shaped" and that he must "punish" the one who set it alight. Although he has been convinced by the young women that he can stay "a bit longer," his plans to settle in are suddenly thwarted by the arrival of Sir Lancelot, who insists that he is in great "peril" and must leave at once. Thus, Galahad is (reluctantly) spirited away from Castle Anthrax, much to the chagrin of the young women who were eager for him to stay longer.

The lessons we glean from this scene are a little easier to identify than those described in previous chapters, but that does not make them any less important. Let's bear in mind what's really happened to Galahad for a moment. In his quest to find the Holy Grail, he has literally stumbled across a castle where

150 young women are living by themselves. This imagery suggests that this might be a convent, but it is, in fact, something completely different. However, Galahad's dedication to the Quest means that he must first seek the Holy Grail. When he discovers that the image he saw in the wilderness that led him to the castle was not the Grail but instead a "Grail-shaped" beacon, he realizes that he's hit a dead end. And this is where we learn our lesson from Sir Galahad: You may have unanticipated opportunities when you realize you've hit a dead end.

While Steven Spielberg was making a film adaptation of a popular novel in the 1970s, he had all kinds of problems with a major special effect in the film. In this case, the problematic effects of his constant failures cost him a lot of money and frustration. The production team was so bent out of shape they renamed the object after Spielberg's lawyer – Bruce.

Bruce was extremely uncooperative whenever Spielberg needed him to work on cue. Finally, Spielberg realized that Bruce wasn't the key effect that was going to make the film work. Instead, the effect would be the anticipation of Bruce and what Bruce represented that would either make or break the movie. Spielberg realized that he could film sections of Bruce rather than as a whole and, by the time the audience saw Bruce at the end of the film, the sense of anticipation would have built up so much that he figured he could probably get them to believe almost anything he wanted.

If you haven't figured it out by now, Bruce was the name of the mechanical shark that appears in the movie *Jaws* (although our die-hard Monty Python fans may be thinking of a completely different Bruce). There were, in fact, three different mechanical sharks that were collectively referred to as "Bruce." But it didn't matter which shark was being used; Bruce constantly sank, and the film crew could never get the takes it needed to make the movie work. Spielberg figured out that the movie wasn't about the shark; it was about people being terrified of the shark. He only needed to create an image in the mind of the audience and, when the shark was finally revealed, all would fall into place. This strategy was so successful that the movie is widely accepted as the first-ever summer blockbuster to gross hundreds of millions of dollars. To this day, the film is considered one of the great American motion pictures of all time.

Spielberg's unanticipated opportunity was to discover how psychology and emotion could have a greater impact than special effects in his future movies. And that formula has worked for Steven Spielberg ever since.

There are, of course, many other examples we could discuss regarding the unanticipated opportunities we might find when we think we've hit a dead end. Rather than spending a lot of time going over numerous examples, however, I think the important thing to remember is that we must keep our eyes open so we can notice the opportunities that present themselves when we think we have reached a dead end. Sir Galahad does exactly that when he announces, "I could stay a bit longer" to the maidens at Castle Anthrax. Galahad suddenly realizes what he's truly stumbled onto and has begun to recognize the enormous opportunities before him: a chance to spend time with 150 young women after they have decided that Zoot must be punished for lighting the Grail-shaped beacon. He is in a rather enviable position that any knight (or bachelor of any era for that matter) would appreciate. Unfortunately for Sir Galahad, Sir Lancelot appears from nowhere and drags him away, thinking he is rescuing Sir Galahad from a "perilous" fate. This brings us to the second lesson to be learned from The Tale of Sir Galahad: Others may prevent you from taking advantage of unforeseen opportunities when they arise.

Many of us have friends and colleagues who wish us nothing but the best and have some very good intentions (remember what the Bible says about "good intentions") but tend to step in or be overprotective at the worst possible times. Some colleagues and so-called "friends" may, in fact, deliberately want to keep us from experiencing things that they themselves cannot experience first-hand. Think about the actions of a person who "forgot" to forward a message to you from an important client or a college roommate who volunteered to "look after" your new car while you were away on a weekend camping trip. And I'm sure, if I were to go out and interview people about the time they wanted to meet someone socially, the romantic examples of how a friend got in the way – either their friend or the person of interest's friend – could no doubt fill an entire volume. Sadly, these types of things happen more than we would like to admit.

Let us consider for a moment how this is not just about keeping you from experiencing pleasant things. Doctoral students must endure a bit of intellectual torture known as writing a dissertation. While dissertation writing is not high on the list of enjoyable things doctoral students must do, there is usually a time limit to complete a doctoral program, and taking advantage of the time available to complete a dissertation is critical. A close friend of mine in Nevada spent many hours in graduate school fighting what seemed like a never-ending battle to complete his dissertation. One of the largest obstacles he had to overcome was his roommate, a law student. My friend likes to claim that he never once saw his roommate crack open a textbook or study for an exam. Now, I am sure that the roommate did these things, but my friend said he never saw him doing anything along the lines of what is normally associated with attending law school, like studying or camping out in the law library. Also, my friend noted that his roommate seemed to go out of town on road trips every weekend. I was under the impression that the roommate traveled more for fun during his time in law school than he had as an undergraduate.

On those occasions, when my friend was in the groove and making significant headway on one particularly daunting section or another of his dissertation, the roommate would call from a local bar or coffee shop and suggest that he take a break. However, the breaks he had in mind weren't of the Starbucks variety. No, apparently the roommate was prone to making frequent suggestions to take weekend trips to Los Angeles or to Lake Tahoe for skiing or kayaking. My friend consistently balked at every suggestion. He always made the comment that the roommate would respond that he could take just "one break." He could afford to leave the dissertation alone for 48 hours – it wouldn't kill him. He was working too hard. He needed to relax a little bit.

What my friend and I knew, of course, and the roommate never seemed to comprehend (although I did try to explain it to him on more than one occasion) was that doctoral students had no guarantee that their studies would continue to be funded in the following year. My friend considered it imperative to finish his dissertation within an allotted timeframe so that he would not have to borrow any money to continue his doctoral studies. The fact that his studies had been funded thus far was no guarantee they would continue to be funded in the future. My friend also knew that, if he took one "break," this would most likely lead to other "breaks," and he would fall further and further behind in his attempt to complete his dissertation by the deadline he had set. The roommate did not have any malicious intent but, had my friend taken him up on his frequent suggestions to "take a break," he would probably have missed the opportunity to effectively use valuable time on weekends and in the evenings to finish a major requirement of the doctoral program. He would tell you that, no matter how much fun he might have had at the beach in Oxnard or how many people he might have met on the slopes near Tahoe, he still didn't think it would have made up for the lost time, effort and progress needed to complete the dissertation.

This example doesn't quite depict Sir Lancelot barging into Castle Anthrax, but had my friend given in to his roommate's pressure, he may not have a doctoral degree today. By the same token, had Sir Galahad been able to "stay just a bit longer" at Castle Anthrax, I suspect that he would have had a very good time, but would have missed the opportunity to continue in his quest for the Holy Grail!

So, remember the lessons learned from The Tale of Sir Galahad: 1) You may have unanticipated opportunities when you find out you've hit a dead end and 2) others may prevent you from taking advantage of those opportunities.

CHAPTER NINE

THE LESSON OF
THE KNIGHTS WHO SAY NI

*"You must return here with a shrubbery or else you
will never pass through this wood alive."*
-The Leader of the Knights Who Say Ni

Now, before we get into this next chapter, I must admit
that I find the Knights Who Say Ni to be much too silly
(the late Graham Chapman would approve, I think),
but I do get a lot of mileage out of them and their tale
within the film, so I will continue to refer to them, since
their story provides some good lessons.

The closest we come to sheer terror in *Monty
Python and the Holy Grail* is about midway through
the film when King Arthur and Sir Bedevere are

traveling through a fog filled forest and see quick flashes of dark figures darting here and there. The absolute fear in Arthur's eyes is unmistakable. They are then forced to face the creatures that frighten them so. Coming face-to-face with the Knights Who Say Ni, Arthur, and Bedevere are given a chance to escape certain doom if they appease the Knights Who Say Ni by bringing them a shrubbery. Once the Knights have made their desires clear, they command Arthur and Bedevere to return with the shrubbery. If they fail to do so, they will not pass through the forest alive.

Once again, I can hear many of you (just like my former students used to) asking, what's the lesson you think you've found in this? You've stayed with me this far, and I promise not to let you down.

How many times have we approached something with a sense of dread and anxiety only to find out that the "something" wasn't as bad as we thought it would be? The best example I can probably give as a former academic is that of the dreaded comprehensive final exam. So many times, my students worried apocalyptically about these most awful of tests. Church attendance rises remarkably, especially at Southeastern Conference institutions, on the Sunday prior to final exam week. There will be much wailing and gnashing of teeth before the exam, but once the exams are past, those who have completed them stop and say to themselves, "Well, that wasn't so bad after all." What about having to meet the parents of a person you are interested in romantically? Of course, the younger you are, the more nerve-wracking this event tends to be. But I think that most of us discover that, despite our nervousness, *most of the time* the parents of the person we love tend to be supportive because their child is happy.

My point here is this: We often approach things, having a huge misperception about how they really are. Think about stereotyping for a second. Whenever I mention Alabama to people who have never visited this state or don't really know anyone from there, the reactions are almost always negative. Alabama is perceived to be a backwards state that is run by people who have little or no education and live in a cultural vacuum. Nothing could be further from the truth. Alabama is a beautiful place with excellent universities, a fine cultural tradition as exemplified by the Alabama Shakespeare Festival and the Birmingham Museum of Art, and a heritage that includes some of America's greatest technological and military triumphs, illustrated by NASA's Marshall Space Flight Center in Huntsville and the Battleship *Alabama* in Mobile. But stereotypical viewpoints often handicap what we are willing to accept as true based on our perceptions.

Take a moment and think about the last person about whom you changed your opinion. Did you possibly have a negative opinion of this person and then later decide that this was off-base or did you think someone was really top-notch but then decided the opposite was true? Did you tell others that the person was not all that bad? Or did you find yourself hoping that you would never to have to deal with him or her again anytime soon?

Sadly, we frequently make misjudgments in our microwave society. Too often, people do not take the time to get all available information before making a decision. It's this rush to judgment and failure to think critically that is often at the root of our misjudgments and the misunderstandings that we face in daily life. Still, when we take the time to examine things and apply our critical thinking skills, we often discover that they do not present the obstacle we once thought they did.

The Knights Who Say Ni are feared by Arthur and Bedevere (whose fear is based largely upon rumor and innuendo), but when the Knights make their demand for a shrubbery, Arthur is immediately baffled and must question them. It is an absolutely ridiculous request and completely unexpected coming from a group of allegedly terrifying forest dwellers. We, the audience, recognize immediately that the Knights Who Say Ni aren't all they're cracked up to be, but Arthur and Bedevere will only figure this out when they return with the shrubbery.

The important thing to remember here is that perceptions can be misleading, and leaders have a responsibility to understand a situation before passing judgment. If you, as a leader, use good critical thinking skills, examine the available evidence and ask questions to find answers you don't have, then you will have a much better chance of avoiding situations in which misperceptions can hinder your ability to make good decisions. And, who knows, by avoiding or eliminating poor perceptions, you might find sunnier paths on which to travel.

The lesson of The Knights Who Say Ni is an important one for leaders to remember: Our perceptions can be wrong, and sometimes we overreact to things we don't completely understand.

Chapter Ten

The Lesson of Sir Lancelot's Rescue

"Well, you see, the thing is I thought your son was a lady."
- Sir Lancelot

One of the most important lessons that we can learn from watching *Monty Python and the Holy Grail* comes from one of the most over-the-top scenes in the entire film. The lesson we learn from this scene has great potential to save us embarrassment and help us avoid miscalculation and costly mistakes that might perhaps take much time and resources to correct.

While riding through a forest, Sir Lancelot and Concord receive a message from someone who claims to be held captive in the tall tower of Swamp Castle. Lancelot, determined to make a daring rescue, sets off in haste to save the person in distress. Storming the castle on his own, Lancelot wreaks havoc by killing or maiming scores of people who have assembled there for a wedding. Upon arriving in the upper-most chamber of the tall tower, he kneels before the sender of the message, proclaims himself to be a humble servant, but suddenly realizes that he is not rescuing a damsel in distress (as he had hoped) but rather a reluctant groom who does not wish to marry the princess his father has chosen for him. Once the father arrives on the scene, he discovers Lancelot's identity and makes a vain attempt to set things right while attempting to rid himself of his son and surreptitiously adopting Sir Lancelot. And, of course, in the finest tradition of Monty Python, it all goes horribly wrong.

How many times have we received word about something and decided to take immediate action without really considering the consequences of what we might be getting ourselves into? This is exactly what Sir Lancelot has done here. He's so eager to have his moment of glory that he decides to rush off and rescue the sender of the note without really thinking the matter through and, as a result, he ends up confused and disappointed.

How many of us are eager to make a big sale, volunteer for a project that might land us that important promotion we've been waiting for, buy something excessively expensive but is briefly "on sale," or go on a blind date because we really want to find that right person? And when we go out and do these things without knowing all we need to know about the situation we've gotten into, how often does the sale fall through, the volunteer effort go unnoticed, the expenditure regretted, or the blind date fail to go as well as we would have liked?

The thing is this: We are often guilty of misinterpreting the messages we receive because of our preset notions and predispositions, or the wants and desires that we wish to have fulfilled. Imagine for a moment that you work for a Fortune 100 company in a lower level position but wish to move into management. Imagine that your immediate boss comes to you and says: "The vice president for sales really thinks it would be a good idea for you to help out with the Billingsley account this weekend." Would you eagerly volunteer to help out with this account without finding out why the VP for sales wants you involved? What if you had plans to go to a hockey game with your friends? What if your son was in a school play, and you had promised to attend, or your daughter had a piano recital? What if it was your anniversary? Would you be the person who asks, "How high?" because someone with immediate authority over you has said, "Jump!"? Or would you be too scared to ask, "Why?" due to fear that you might be judged as "unwilling to help out?"

One of the things I tried to teach the students every semester during my career as a professor was how to develop better critical thinking skills. All too often when people receive messages, they fail to use proper critical thinking skills to correctly interpret those messages. Think about your personal biases for a moment. We all have things that we either like or dislike. These likes and dislikes can have a large impact on how we interpret messages from others and, hence, respond to those messages. Let's say that it's early October, and you are a huge Boston Red Sox fan who lives in Orlando, Florida. Imagine now that you decide to call out and order a pizza for dinner that evening. Your phone conversation is pleasant, and you are certain that you will receive a piping hot pizza delivered with a smile to your door in a relatively short period of time. Now, let's throw a few variables into the mix. Your pizza arrives 55 minutes after you have made the phone call, you are now exceedingly hungry, and the pizza delivery guy arrives at your front door wearing a New York Yankees ball cap and T-shirt. And the Yankees beat the Red Sox for the American League Pennant just a few days earlier. How will you react? And, what about the guy who delivers your pizza? What if he's never delivered to your house before, was caught in traffic and apologized to you for being late? How will you treat him and how much will you tip him so he can buy groceries and have some food next week?

One thing that many of us overlook is the impersonal nature of communication. This is particularly true in written communication. Sir Lancelot has made several assumptions (which are completely fair for the setting of the movie – one would expect a note of distress to be sent by a lady but not a man!) that he relies on while interpreting the message that asks for help. His assumptions are completely incorrect, but he is doing his best to interpret the message with limited information. He knows the sender's general circumstances, but has no idea that the note has been written by someone named "Herbert."

Too many of us base our assumptions on what we read or hear from others without having access or paying attention to the elements of nonverbal communication that are essential to understanding and interpreting messages from others. Consider e-mail messages for a moment. How often have you read an e-mail message from someone you don't know very well and decided that you didn't like the "tone" of the message? Think about that for a moment. Tone is widely accepted as a vocal quality. It is something generally interpreted by the ear. So, can an e-mail message have a tone? Some will no doubt argue that an e-mail message can have a tone, but I suggest that it's not the written words that carry the tone, but our perceptions of the sender and our moods at the moment we read a message that alters our interpretation of those words and causes us to imprint the notion of tone onto the message itself. Try this experiment: Find a message in your e-mail box that you aren't too happy about and print it out. Once you've printed out the message, change the name of the sender to someone you really like or just black out the original sender's name and e-mail address completely. Walk away for twenty minutes and then re-read it. Has your interpretation of what is written on the page changed? If your answer was no, then put the message away for a couple of days and come back to it and try again.

Messages are often misinterpreted for a myriad of reasons that go beyond personal biases and emotional influences. Verbal communication, especially of the written variety, is highly impersonal. Studies have consistently shown that most communication – some studies suggest it may be as high as 93% – is nonverbal in nature. We are heavily reliant on things like facial expressions, physical distance, hand gestures, posture, eye contact and even color and smells to back up the words we use.

If you don't believe in the importance of nonverbal communication take one look at flight deck operations aboard aircraft carriers. Arguably, the flight deck of an aircraft carrier is one of the noisiest working environments in the world. Regular verbal communication is practically impossible given all the noise. But with a system of hand signals, teams of workers, who wear differently colored jerseys to denote the different jobs they do, are able to perform a complex series of operations without speaking to one another. There are loudspeakers that can broadcast messages to those on the flight deck, but these are more often used to give directional announcements rather than orchestrate the work that goes on every time a plane is launched or recovered aboard a carrier. Without effective nonverbal communication, these critical jobs at sea would not get done.

Nonverbal communication can speak volumes beyond words and, in many cases, can be completed infinitely faster than verbal communication. Gestures and other nonverbal cues such as hand signals or a look can be much easier to understand and more rapidly understood in many cases than the words one might try to use while formulating a message. I think it's safe to say that it's highly unfortunate that Sir Lancelot didn't receive any nonverbal communication cues from the sender of the note, for if he had gotten these, there would have been a lot less explaining to do.

Let's also consider the impact of noise on the receiver's ability to receive and interpret messages. Noise is anything that can distract you from correctly interpreting a message. The concept of serial distortion is closely related to noise. While you may not recognize the term, you know exactly what serial distortion is. Think back to when you were in elementary school, and you played the "Silent Post" game in which, on one side of the room, the teacher whispered a message like "Cookie Monster is coming to visit on Friday" into the ear of the student sitting next to him or her. That student then turns and whispers the message to the next student, who turns and whispers to the next student, and so on and so on, until it reaches the last child in the classroom who announces that "Fried cookies are on the menu at the monster truck rally today!" Once noise has entered into the communication cycle, it can become exceedingly difficult to interpret messages correctly.

Communication is critical to the success of any endeavor and, while words matter, we must always remember that communication encompasses much more than words. We must always consider how our cultural conditioning, personal and collective experiences, perceptions, and biases can impact our interpretations of and responses to messages. There's a reason that most executives insist that employees in their organizations have outstanding communication skills.

The lesson of Sir Lancelot's rescue is critically important for all leaders: Messages can be (and often are) easily misinterpreted; beware of inserting biases into messages and, if vital nonverbal communication cues are missing,

make sure you have all the information you really need before rushing headlong into what may be a big mistake.

CHAPTER ELEVEN

THE LESSON OF
ROGER THE SHRUBBER

*"Oh, what sad times are these when passing ruffians
can say "ni" at will to old ladies."*
- Roger the Shrubber

As noted earlier, I've gotten a lot of mileage out of the
subplot surrounding the Knights Who Say Ni. While
we dealt earlier with the initial encounter between
Arthur, Bedevere and the Knights Who Say Ni, we
should now visit the man who made the undoing of the
Knights Who Say Ni possible. Although his appearance
in the film is very brief, Roger the Shrubber is an
important character for our purposes, so we should

give him some proper attention. Let's review the scene when Arthur and Bedevere happen to meet him. Finding themselves in a village, Arthur and Bedevere chance upon an old woman and ask her if she knows where they can find a shrubbery. She insists there are no shrubberies in the village, but Arthur and Bedevere refuse to believe it and begin saying "ni" to her. While this happens, a man who says he is called "Roger the Shrubber" stops to chastise them for their behavior. Not thinking before acting, Bedevere attempts to say "ni" to Roger before Arthur restrains him.

Like the other scenes in the movie I have discussed, this one also provides some valuable lessons for leaders. Arthur and Bedevere have been tasked with finding a shrubbery that the Knights Who Say Ni will like. This is apparently a difficult task for them, as they have resorted to harassing an old woman who challenges them to "do their worst" rather than offer them any assistance. It is only sheer luck that Roger passes by and encounters Arthur and Bedevere harassing the old woman. And it is also by chance that he is so bothered by their behavior that he stops to say something about it. Roger's characterization of Arthur and Bedevere as "passing ruffians" doesn't even faze the King, who seems a bit embarrassed that he has resorted to "terror" tactics to get what he wants. Roger's timely appearance brings us to our first lesson from this scene: Opportunities often present themselves when you least expect them.

Now, you may be asking yourself: How this lesson is different from the Lesson of Sir Galahad? Remember that with Sir Galahad we were looking at an opportunity that appeared when an apparent dead end had been reached. What we're looking at here is a chance encounter or situation that brings you something completely unexpected. There are numerous historical examples of how people benefited from things that they didn't expect to find or create. Levi Strauss didn't go to California to sell jeans. He was trying to sell tents to the miners of the California Gold Rush. Denim didn't work so well as tent material, but he discovered it was surprisingly great for making trousers. The alleged invention of the ice cream cone at the 1904 St. Louis World's Fair was as much of a godsend to the poor ice cream sellers who couldn't keep up with washing ice cream dishes as it was to the waffle vendor, who wasn't selling much of anything thanks to the demand for ice cream. Neither was expecting the other to be able to provide a solution to their individual problems, but the unexpected opportunity led to one of the greatest successes of the 20th century. I don't pretend to have an explanation for why serendipitous events happen, but because they do, it's important to appreciate their value when they come along and take advantage of them before the opportunity is gone.

Ironically, it is often when we think that we have failed at something, but are not quite at a dead end, that an opportunity we weren't expecting comes along. Just look at the work of any successful inventor for proof of this statement. How many things did Thomas Edison invent? And how many failures did he have? The genesis of some of our best ideas and greatest opportunities often arise from failures. Remember the famous words of Admiral James T. Kirk, spoken to Lieutenant Saavik in *Star Trek II: The Wrath of Khan* when she wanted to know how he had defeated the Kobayashi Maru scenario: "We learn by doing."

But taking advantage of unexpected opportunities isn't the only lesson we learn from this scene, and leaders need to pay attention. In the final seconds of the scene, before we jump back to the Knights Who Say Ni, Arthur and Bedevere provide us with a brief flash of something that is supremely important, which is our second lesson gained from this scene: Don't threaten those who offer you solutions. Sir Bedevere, in a brief moment of belligerency, shouts "ni" at Roger but is restrained by King Arthur before any serious damage can be done.

People are often threatened by those who offer solutions to problems for various reasons. Some people fear losing influence or to change their situation or status quo. Think of small children who go to the doctor for vaccinations. Generally, they do not like being stuck with a needle and will cry and wail when the needle appears even before being stuck. But we all know that the doctor is only trying to prevent the child from contracting an illness which may endanger the child's life.

When new people appear in an organization who have new or different ways of approaching problems, how are those people treated? If you are a leader, are you setting the appropriate example for others when interacting with this person? Do you act like King Arthur in that you try to restrain those who act like Sir Bedevere or do you stand by and do nothing? As we will see in the lesson of Tim the Enchanter, no one dared to threaten Tim because he appeared to have great power by using controlled explosions, but when King Arthur and his knights didn't like what Tim had to say, they ridiculed him and ended up in the wrong. Had they shown Tim more respect, might the outcome have been different? Only the film's writers can really answer that question, but the point is this: Treating others well and with respect can often work to your benefit. Arthur restrained Bedevere and got a shrubbery to present the Knights Who Say Ni.

Without followers, one cannot be a leader, but leaders have a responsibility to treat their followers with respect and show them that their contributions and opinions are valued. Every stakeholder in an organization has the potential to provide something unexpected, and perhaps even a solution to a problem. Be open to their contributions even if they aren't what you were expecting or aren't necessarily your first choices, but please, try to avoid saying "ni;" it's just too silly.

Always remember the lessons from Roger the Shrubber:

1) Opportunities often present themselves unexpectedly.
2) Don't threaten those who offer you solutions.

Chapter Twelve

The Lesson of the Knights Who Say ????

"We are now no longer the Knights Who Say Ni."
-The leader of The Knights Who 'til Recently Said Ni

Returning to the Knights Who Say Ni brings us to our next lesson in leadership. When Arthur and Bedevere encountered these Knights while passing through the forest, they were given the task to find a shrubbery and return to them with it. Arthur and Bedevere succeed in this task, but when they return with the shrubbery, they encounter a situation they were not expecting and are reunited with Sir Robin (who proves what we already knew about the Knights Who Say Ni, i.e., that they are not really that scary). Once Arthur returns with a shrubbery from Roger, the Knights Who Say Ni express their happiness but inform Arthur that there is a problem. They say they are no longer the Knights

Who Say Ni. They have changed their name and, furthermore, they demand another shrubbery and that Arthur and Bedevere chop down the tallest tree in the forest with a herring. Arthur refuses to do so and inadvertently utters the one word the Knights cannot stand to hear: "it." Apparently, utterances of "it" sends the Knights into fits. "Brave" Sir Robin appears and continues to say "it," much to the Knights' chagrin. Finally, Arthur has decided they have had enough and commands Bedevere and Robin to leave, while the Knights Who No Longer Say Ni writhe in agony next to their new shrubbery.

Now, in this scene, you may think that King Arthur and Sir Bedevere realize that the "Knights Who 'til Recently Said Ni" aren't as scary as they once thought (which is completely true), however, something far more important is illustrated here. And I would like to point out for the record that "brave" Sir Robin (who is actually a complete coward) was absolutely not afraid of the Knights Who Say Ni, even though Arthur and Bedevere were initially terrified of them. Given Sir Robin's nature, my main question is why isn't he scared of them? My guess is that he has no idea who they are and, therefore, has no reason to be afraid of them.

So, what has really happened here? Arthur and Bedevere encountered the Knights Who Say Ni while traveling through the misty forest. The Knights commanded Arthur and Bedevere to bring them a shrubbery and stated that, if they did not, they would not pass through the forest alive. Arthur and Bedevere bring the shrubbery, which the Knights apparently like. Then, the Knights announce they have changed their identity and assign another absurd task. Arthur refuses, and the Knights whine like toddlers and ask, "oh please?" Arthur explains that their task is impossible and utters the word "it," which the Knights can't bear to hear. Sir Robin arrives saying "it" in almost every sentence, thereby, torturing the Knights. Arthur becomes frustrated and leaves with Sir Bedevere and Sir Robin to continue their quest.

So, what is the earth-shattering development in this scene that is so important? Quite simply, the fact that the Knights Who Say Ni have announced publicly that they are no longer the Knights Who Say Ni; they are now The Knights Who Say Icky Icky Icky Icky Batang Zoom Room (or something like that). They have, in fact, attempted to change their identity and have done so in a way that is overly complicated and completely absurd. And that's the important development: the attempt to change one's identity.

The desire to reinvent one's self is nothing new. History is replete with examples of rulers, organizations and entire societies which have decided that they need a makeover and change their image for one reason or another. Change can be a good thing. Human beings are complex and dynamic creatures

78

who, in many cases, are easily bored and often weary of the status quo. The emperors of Ancient Rome often illustrated this point nicely, for example, why else would Emperor Titus have flooded the Colosseum and staged reenactments of famous naval battles? We mostly associate the Colosseum with gladiators and those famous, yet clearly one-sided battles between the early Christians and some rather peckish lions. But one must be very careful when attempting to rebrand.

In autumn 2010, the popular clothing retailer The Gap decided it needed a fresh new logo. They abandoned their iconic blue square upon which the simple name "GAP" was centered in white and to which their loyal customers were accustomed, developing a similar but not identical new logo. The backlash resulting from the logo change forced the company to abandon the new marketing effort and return to the classic, much-loved emblem. This case in point illustrates that it is difficult to change an established image. What makes an image so attractive to many is that it appears to have a solid foundation of credibility. And what many people fail to consider is that credibility is not something you can buy or develop overnight. It takes time, effort and patience to establish credibility. In my lectures, in which this important notion was discussed, I often likened the development of credibility to building a house. If you're going to build a solid house that will last for decades, then you have to use the right materials, check your work carefully and not take irresponsible shortcuts. Conversely, while building credibility takes time, it can be ruined in moments. You need only look as far as examples of long serving politicians whose careers are destroyed in hours due to a scandal that appears online and goes viral before the story hits the 24-hour cable news channels that evening to see my point.

Since we're on this topic, credibility is what I like to call a "critical key point." It doesn't really matter who you are or what you do; if you have credibility, others will take you seriously. But if you have taken actions that have eroded or eliminated your credibility, then you may simply become the equivalent of the boy who cried wolf. Take, for instance, former NFL quarterback Brett Favre. When he announced his retirement from the Green Bay Packers in 2008, people took him seriously, and we had thought that he was done playing the game. Then, he announced he was coming back. He spent a year playing for the New York Jets. Then, he announced he was retiring... again. Then, he came back and played for the Minnesota Vikings. Then, he announced he was retiring... again. When his last announcement came in late 2010, my reaction was "who will he be playing for in the fall?" Quite simply, Favre's statements about retirement had lost any credibility for me because his actions failed to consistently back up his words. Talk is cheap. Seriously. If you truly want others to believe in a change you are making, you must back up all the talk with consistent and reliable actions. Altering your course and backtracking will do nothing to help you build credibility with those you seek to influence.

However, if you feel that you must change your image to the world, make sure that your efforts will be seriously appreciated and that your credibility is sound, otherwise you may find yourself, like the Knights Who No Longer Say Ni, in the forest on your own (individually or collectively, of course) while others go on past, ignoring just how annoying you've really become.

The lesson of The Knights Who No Longer Say Ni is important to those who are passionate about change: Be very careful if you choose to change your identity; if you don't do it properly, others may no longer take you seriously.

Chapter Thirteen

The Wisdom of Tim the Enchanter

"Look at the bones!"
- Tim the Enchanter

Probably the most action-packed scene in *Monty Python and the Holy Grail* also provides a lesson that many of my students couldn't recognize when I presented it to them. Following an animated sequence in which Arthur and the knights have rested for a year, the expedition encounters a man in a rocky landscape who is setting off powerful explosions, much to the amazement of Arthur and his knights. They soon learn he is an enchanter named Tim. Not wanting to miss an opportunity to gather information from this man about where they might find the Holy Grail, Arthur decides to ask for his help. Tim agrees but delivers to Arthur a stern warning. He will take them to a location where they can discover the final resting place of the Holy Grail, but it is guarded by a deadly creature that has killed scores of men, whose bones lay strewn about the ground. Tim takes Arthur and his knights to the Cave of Caerbannog, but upon their arrival, pauses to see if the dreaded guardian of the cave is about. Before the party can proceed ahead, Tim stops them, saying that it is too late. At this point, the creature, which looks like a small white rabbit, appears. When asked if the monster is behind the rabbit, Tim explains that the rabbit is what has caused all the death and destruction. Arthur and his knights immediately lose all faith in Tim and begin to ridicule him, refusing to believe anything else he has to say. Arthur then sends one of his knights out to clear the way, but the knight is immediately decapitated by the rabbit. Arthur and the knights are shocked, and the tables are turned as Tim begins to mock them for doubting him. A decision is made to charge the rabbit, resulting in even more casualties. The party is then abandoned by Tim, who walks off laughing at their futile attempts to slay the killer rabbit. Finally, Arthur calls for the Holy Hand Grenade of Antioch to dispatch the creature. The rabbit is killed, and the party proceeds into the cave.

The central problem in this scene is that Arthur and the knights refuse to accept what they have been told by an outsider, who happens to know much more about the dangers they will face. Despite having been dramatically warned before they arrive at the entrance of the cave, they still ignore the obvious and rely on their own assumptions about what might or might not be dangerous. Even though they have seen all the bones of men lying about on the ground, they still choose not to take Tim seriously. Only after witnessing one of their own knights being slain by what they mistakenly believe to be a "harmless little bunny" do they realize the trouble they're in.

How many instances can we recount from business, war, politics and even social settings where people fail to take warnings and advice from others seriously? The main problem that Arthur and his knights have with Tim's warning is that their experience has shown them that a rabbit typically does not display killer instincts. They incorrectly assume that Tim has been exaggerating about the rabbit's homicidal tendencies and overconfidently approach the animal with disastrous results. Even when Tim cries "Look at the bones!" they still refuse to believe what he is telling them.

There is a second problem in this scene (beyond ignoring the advice of an expert) that many refuse to acknowledge. Tim the Enchanter, although an impressive man in that he can demonstrate his mastery over fire and explosions, loses credibility with Arthur and the knights the moment he explains that the rabbit is dangerous. The others refuse to listen to him in large part because he is not a member of their in-group. Arguably, there are times when managers must carefully and critically consider advice from people outside their inner circles. Unfortunately, in many cases, managers will ignore someone outright who doesn't fit their expectations or will make outsiders prove their worth before even considering what they might have to contribute. And, all too often, managers tragically refuse to listen when an outsider tells them something they do not want to hear.

History presents us with a tragic example of management failing (or refusing) to listen to experts. In July 1985, Morton Thiokol engineer Roger Boisjoly wrote a memo to senior managers in which he warned them about a problem with the O-ring seals on the solid rocket boosters of the space shuttle. Boisjoly warned – in writing – that unless the problem was corrected, the result would be loss of human life.

On the evening of January 27, 1986, engineers and managers from Morton Thiokol debated in a conference call with NASA officials at the Marshall Space Flight Center in Huntsville, Alabama about the safety of launching the shuttle *Challenger* in temperatures that were colder than had been expected. The engineers warned management not to launch, but they were ignored and discounted. And, in the end, just 73 seconds after liftoff on January 28, 1986, *Challenger* exploded, killing all seven astronauts on live television. In the investigation that followed, word of Boisjoly's memo leaked to the press and, both NASA and Morton Thiokol were asked hard questions.

Another, even more, devastating aerospace disaster gives us a different perspective on listening to experts. On May 25, 1979, American Airlines Flight 191 departed Chicago's O'Hare International Airport outbound for Los Angeles. Moments after takeoff, the port engine of the McDonnell-Douglas DC-10 separated from the pylon on the underside of the wing, and the aircraft lost control and crashed, killing 273 people. It was the worst aviation-related disaster in the United States prior to the terrorist attacks on September 11, 2001.

In the aftermath of the disaster, former astronaut Pete Conrad, who was then a vice president for McDonnell-Douglas, accepted a request from company head James McDonnell to investigate the matter on behalf of the company. Conrad was asked for a variety of reasons – he was a well-known personality at the time for having walked on the moon during the Apollo 12 mission and for flying in the Gemini and Skylab Projects. His face was familiar to millions of Americans because of an American Express commercial he had filmed in the 1970s. But, more importantly to McDonnell-Douglas, Conrad was not only an accomplished pilot and astronaut, he also held a degree in aeronautical engineering from Princeton University.

As Conrad began his investigation, the National Transportation Safety Board and American Airlines raised objections and concerns regarding his participation. They were concerned that he would not be objective, but he went about his own work while fighting to take an active part in the investigation. While the NTSB and American Airlines were sifting through the wreckage of the DC-10, Conrad relied on his own expertise and located the cause of the crash weeks before the government and airline investigators. The cause of the crash was due to shortcuts that had been taken by American Airlines maintenance teams while servicing the engines. Rather than removing the engines from their wing pylons, forklifts were placed under the engines to support them while the service was done. This resulted in fractures which ultimately led to the failure in Flight 191. Conrad immediately notified the inspection teams, and similar fractures were found on other DC-10s at American and Continental Airlines.

Conrad looked where others did not – at the billable hours for maintenance – to find the solution. Eventually, his findings were accepted by the NTSB investigators and procedures were changed to make sure that similar incidents would not occur in the future. But the fact remains that initially Conrad's expertise was ignored before his conclusions were accepted.

But let's return to *Monty Python*. Tim's reaction to the failure of Arthur and the knights to defeat the killer rabbit should not be surprising. How many of us, after watching others do something we have told them not to do, must bite our tongues to not say "I told you so!"? What is telling, however, is that Tim leaves Arthur and the knights to figure out how to solve the problem themselves. He just laughs and walks off, unwilling to give any more advice or warnings after the way he's been treated. Arthur is forced to consider his other options and must call upon a priest traveling with him to bring forth the Holy Hand Grenade of Antioch to kill the rabbit.

Now, do we really blame Arthur for not completely believing what Tim had to tell him about the rabbit? Based on everyday experience and common sense, the obvious answer is no. But this is *Monty Python*! I know they weren't expecting the Spanish Inquisition, but given Tim's insistence and the physical evidence of the bones in front of the cave, a little bit of critical thinking might have gone a long way toward averting a disaster and expending limited resources (it's probably safe to assume that there was only one Holy Hand Grenade of Antioch) to solve the problem. So, before leaping into a situation you may not totally understand, it may be wise to listen to the Tim the

Enchanters of the world. Examine the evidence before you, listen to the advice of those familiar with the situation, consider all variables that could impact your decision and ask questions when there is uncertainty.

The Wisdom of Tim the Enchanter is important for every good leader to remember: Listen to the experts when they try to tell you there are problems.

CHAPTER FOURTEEN

THE LESSON OF
THE BRIDGE KEEPER

"What do you mean? African or European?"
- King Arthur

Ironically, we have a return to the issue of swallows (no coconuts on this one) toward the end of the film when Arthur and his knights meet the Keeper of the Bridge of Death. The Bridge Keeper asks each traveler three questions, and he must answer them correctly, or he will be cast into the Gorge of Eternal Peril.

Arthur and the knights clearly understand the challenge that faces them in the form of the Bridge Keeper's questions. If they answer the questions correctly, they will be able to safely cross the gorge.

After watching Sir Lancelot answer three very easy questions, Sir Robin steps forward, only to be foiled by a difficult question that he clearly hadn't anticipated. Sir Galahad's indecision in answering the Bridge Keeper's third question caused him to be cast into the gorge after Sir Robin.

Finally, Arthur steps forward and easily answers the first two questions and then inadvertently thwarts the Bridge Keeper by asking him to clarify his question about the airspeed velocity of an unladen swallow. Once the Bridge Keeper has acknowledged that he doesn't know which species of swallow is referred to in the question, he falls victim to his own trap and is himself cast into the Gorge of Eternal Peril. Who among us expected King Arthur to foil the Bridge Keeper by bringing up this trivial point which was raised at the beginning of the film? Even more to Arthur's credit, when Sir Bedevere asks how he knows so much about swallows, rather than recount the entire brutal encounter with the castle guards, Arthur maintains his cool and composure as if he's had the knowledge all along.

The lesson from this scene is an important one that anyone attempting to reach a goal should bear in mind: Being unprepared can lead to disastrous consequences. How many times have sales people lost an important deal because they were not prepared for a prospective client's resistance? How often do projects fail to meet deadlines and budget requirements because managers and planners didn't account for contingencies? How many job seekers have blown interviews because they didn't properly research the organization that was interviewing them?

The iPhone and iPad are incredibly popular and prolific technologies that have become daily fixtures in the 21st century, but how many of us remember the Apple Newton? In the early 1990s, Apple began work on the first generation of PDAs that were supposed to change the way people used computers. Unfortunately, Apple pulled the plug on the Newton shortly after it had been introduced into the market; however, the company retained and improved upon the technology. Today, personal computing products from Apple abound. If Apple had been fully prepared, however, we might still be using Newtons rather than iPads.

In the film *Miracle* (a dramatization of the US Olympic Hockey Team's 1980 victory at the Lake Placid Games), Coach Herb Brooks (played by actor Kurt Russell) tells his assistant that he isn't looking for the best players; he's looking for the right ones. Both in the movie and in real life, Herb Brooks understood the realities of being prepared for the Soviets. Being prepared meant that Brooks had to consider all the options, recognize the obstacles and be ready to improvise when necessary to achieve the goal: to win the Gold Medal in Hockey against the best team in the world. Those of us who are old enough to remember that historic victory know that it was just what the country needed at the time. With the losses sustained in Vietnam, the trauma of Watergate, 52 of our fellow citizens being held hostage in Tehran, our economy in a free-fall, double digit interest rates, horrific lines at gas stations and Soviet aggression seemingly unchecked, Americans were feeling pretty low. But on that cold day in late February 1980, those 20 kids gave this country what we needed most, exactly when we needed it. And it was all because Herb Brooks knew enough to be prepared.

While it may be impossible to plan for every eventuality or alternative, those who over-prepare are usually much better off at the end of the day than those who underprepare and are caught off-guard by unexpected events. Remember the Keeper of the Bridge of Death? He was completely unprepared for Arthur's questions asking for clarification regarding the airspeed velocity of an "unladen swallow." Because he could not provide the answer Arthur wanted, he ended up falling into his own trap and, presumably, any future travelers could cross the bridge over the Gorge of Eternal Peril in relative safety from that point forward.

The Lesson of the Bridge Keeper is one that you don't have to be a leader to appreciate: Being unprepared can often have disastrous consequences.

Chapter Fifteen

The Moral of the French Knights

"At last, our quest is at an end!"
- King Arthur

After a long and perilous journey, having survived the killer rabbit, the Knights Who Say Ni, harsh weather, cave monsters and even managing to outwit the Keeper of the Bridge of Death, King Arthur and Sir Bedevere (the last survivors of the original party who began the Quest) finally arrive at the Castle Aaarrghh, which is the final resting place of the Holy Grail. Unfortunately, they bump into a few characters with whom they had to deal earlier in the film, namely, the French knights. Refusing Arthur and Bedevere entrance to Castle

Aaarrghh, the French knights taunt the duo and then dump something that looks excessively vile all over them. At the height of their frustration, Arthur and Bedevere walk away, with the French continuing to taunt them as they leave. Once they have reached a reasonable distance, Arthur announces that they will attack immediately. Suddenly, out of nowhere, a massive army appears that begins charging toward the castle, only to have their progress stopped by a local police car. Arthur and Bedevere are arrested and taken away as a policeman halts filming.

At this point, you might be asking "what in the world does this scene have to do with leadership?" If you are, that's okay, because my students were also usually puzzled about that, but I promise you there's a lesson here: conflict is unavoidable. Think about that for a second. What is the longest period you have ever managed to go without having had a conflict over something? Now, it doesn't have to have been a major event that brought people to the point of physical violence, it could have been as simple as a disagreement over who had the right to park beneath the tree in the summer time to get the greatest amount of shade or an argument with the neighbors who played their stereo at a higher volume than you liked.

Politics (and, hence, conflict itself) is rooted in a struggle for scarce resources. In the business world, people often don't recognize that others are struggling to control a myriad of resources – budgets, finances, physical space, distribution channels, office assignments, time, personnel and even who gets the comfy chair. Anywhere a disagreement occurs over something, a conflict also occurs. So yes, conflict is totally unavoidable. However, what's important to remember is that while conflict is a fact of life, it does not have to be a way of life.

Consider for a moment the last time that you had a conflict with someone. How did you handle it? Was your solution constructive or destructive? "Wait a minute," you might be saying – "how in the world can conflict be constructive?" That's a great question. Conflict is not always a bad thing. Many organizations create cultures where dissension and disagreement are almost a capital offense. But we are not living in the time of King Arthur; this is the 21st century. Unfortunately, many executives in the corporate, non-profit, academic and public sectors still act like members of the medieval nobility and dole out punishments to those who refuse to toe the party line and act blindly without question. Now, you don't have to be a malcontent like Dennis the Peasant to get caught up in this situation. Plenty of people, including many who are highly loyal to the organizations they serve, often question the decisions of those in power, when decisions are made that do not seem to make sense. Unfortunately, if those decisions are questioned, such people are all too frequently burned at the stake for doing so!

It is also important for leaders to recognize that attempting to control people's preferences and choices can invite unnecessary conflict. The consequences of attempting to control individual choices that have no impact on how someone works for an organization can be demoralizing to the organization's employees and can also cause image problems for leaders. Now, that's not to say that organizations shouldn't enforce their own codes of ethics or rules for acceptable conduct on the job, but telling someone that you don't like the fact that they are a fan of the Texas Rangers or that they drive a Nissan Versa or Toyota Prius is just asking for trouble. The exception, of course, is Jeremy Clarkson who can tell anyone he likes that he doesn't care for the Toyota Prius. But the individual choices people make and the freedom to make those choices is what helps to define our Western society and brings strength to almost any organization. By forcing their choices on others, leaders are creating destructive points of conflict whether they know it or not.

Okay, so I've gone on about destructive conflict for a while now, but what about constructive conflict? Constructive conflict is actually good because it brings about the opportunity for improvement. Think about the Coca-Cola Company for a moment. In the mid-1980s, Coca-Cola decided to release something they were calling "New Coke." It was a complete disaster.

Consumers revolted. The media had a field day, and "New Coke" became a thing of the past within a few years. Now, why is this an example of "constructive conflict?" If Coca-Cola had not had such passionate consumers who were loyal to a beloved soft drink, Coke might have lost market shares, revenue and their reputation. Coca-Cola learned plenty of lessons from the "New Coke" fiasco that helped make it a better company. Rather than just forcing their product onto the masses, Coke listened to the response and recovered well.

And since we've touched on the topic of listening, it is probably a good idea to discuss something that is closely associated with conflict, namely, the idea of confrontation. Confrontation is a word that can often make people anxious, but this uncomfortable feeling can be avoided. One of the best discussions about constructive conflict can be found in Lani Arredondo's *Communicating Effectively*. Confrontation takes its roots from two Latin words "*con*" and "*frons*" which basically allude to a face-to-face discussion. Unfortunately, "confrontation" has largely negative overtones and so even a hint of the word makes people cringe and, in many cases, can result in procrastination to communicate. If we could return to the more basic meaning of confrontation (i.e., a conversation), then more productive and reasonable dialogs would frequently be the result.

When leaders engage in reasonable dialogue with those who disagree, they would do well to hear out the other side and try to understand the opposing or dissenting viewpoint. If positive change can result from a disagreement or a struggle over scarce resources, then this would be much better than the alternative, which can be disastrous on many different levels. Remember that conflict doesn't have to be the end of the world if only leaders are willing to practice good communication skills (including listening) and occasionally exercise a little empathy.

The Moral of the French Knights is this: Conflict is unavoidable and, although conflict is a fact of life, it does not have to become a way of life.

Conclusion

"You call that an ending?"
- Richard D. Parker

I must have been about 17 years old the first time I saw *Monty Python and the Holy Grail.* I was in high school at the time, and I don't exactly remember where I saw it, but the one thing that always stuck with me about that first viewing was how disappointed I was about the end of the film. Of course, having seen it countless times over the 30 years that have elapsed since I first watched it, I've learned to appreciate the finer aspects of the film, but I think that the conclusion actually provides us with a bonus lesson that – like the Spanish Inquisition – we may not have been expecting. I could call this a carryover from the lesson of Roger the Shrubber, but I'll just get on with it.

All too often, many aspects of life seem to conclude in disappointing ways. Sales deals fall apart, someone misses the last-second shot on goal that would have won the hockey game, a romantic relationship fizzles out or crashes and burns, or you end up failing to study for a final exam because you have an A going into it, but blow the test and end up with a lower grade. Any way you look at it, there's a reason that the British can use the saying "before it all went horribly wrong" in a plethora of situations.

Disappointing endings are another unpleasant fact of life. But do all endings need to be disappointing? No, they don't. We know this because many events in life have ended well.

How we conclude things can also be very telling. We can take the time to conclude something properly, or we can rush to finish something and move on to the next thing. By writing this book, I have attempted to pass along a few life lessons that I have taken away from watching one movie (perhaps once too often). But my goal has been a simple, and I hope an honorable, one, which is to pass on some knowledge that might make a difference. When I became a professor, I did so because I wanted to make a difference in the lives of my students. Similarly, when I left the profession and moved on to a different career, I did so because I felt I could make a greater impact and difference elsewhere. I hope that, while reading this book, I have made you laugh and promoted some deep thinking. Perhaps some of my references are a bit obscure (and I have Dennis Miller's influence to blame for the style of my writing) but, as a writer, my greatest hope is that you've enjoyed the book and can take something memorable away from reading it.

Onward Patsy!!

ACKNOWLEDGEMENTS

There are many people I wish to thank for their help over the years as I worked to draft and refine this text. My wife Alison has been a tremendous supporter, and without her belief in the project, it would not have reached this point; the eminent military historian Dr. Frederick Schneid and Dr. Michael Smith of Georgia Tech's Scheller College of Business, who offered some very good insights and advice on the initial drafts of the manuscript; Dr. Sara Crockett, who spent time copy editing the manuscript; Taylor Kiland, author of *Leadership Lessons from the Hanoi Hilton,* my attorney Alexandra MacKay and my publisher Dennis Lowery who all offered excellent advice and counsel; the creative geniuses at Monty Python who created a masterpiece of British cinema and their representatives in London who safeguard their legacy; and the hundreds of students who, over a 15 year period at five schools, eventually embraced the leadership lessons from *Monty Python and the Holy Grail* and (hopefully) have remembered them.

ABOUT THE AUTHOR

Once upon a time Dr. Richard Parker was a college professor. He earned some degrees, including a Ph.D., from the University of Alabama and later took several more graduate courses with some fine people from McGill University in Montreal. For many years he taught interesting subjects like advertising, public relations, media writing, ethics, leadership communication, and marketing. Early in his teaching career, he discovered that his students could relate to the bland course material if he tied the subject matter back to modern cinema and selected programming from BBC 2. And then one day, he decided to do something completely different.

He joined the U.S. Navy Reserve seeking the chance to serve his country, and like the Queen's Own McKamikaze Highlanders, he left the Ivory Tower behind. Returning home to Nashville, Tennessee he settled down and wrote this book. Having finished, he continues to enjoy British television programming, a good pint from the UK's finest breweries (especially those smaller ones in the Cotswolds), reading history, travels with his wife and wearing Aloha shirts instead of a coat and tie. He was last seen on Wednesday browsing pet stores near Ipswich in search of a Norwegian Blue Parrot, preferably one not pining for the fjords.

BIBLIOGRAPHY

Abrashoff, D. Michael. (2002). *It's Your Ship: Management Techniques from the Best Damn Ship in the Navy*. Business Plus.

Arredondo, Lani. (2000). *Communicating Effectively (The Briefcase Books)*. McGrawHill Education.

Boisjoly, Roger. (2006). *Ethical Decisions – Morton Thiokol and the Space Shuttle Challenger Disaster*. Online at http://www.onlineethics.org/CMS/profpractice/ppes says/thiokolshuttle.aspx

Campbell, Kim Sydow. (2006). *Thinking and Interacting Like a Leader: The TILL System for Effective Interpersonal Communication*. Parlay Enterprises.

Conrad, Nancy and Howard A. Klausner. (2005). *Rocketman: Astronaut Pete Conrad's Incredible Ride to the Moon and Beyond*. NAL Trade.

Honah. Mat. (2013). "Remembering the Apple Newton's Prophetic Failure and Lasting Impact."

Wired. (August 5). Online at https://www.wired.com/2013/08/rememberingthe-apple-newtons-prophetic-failure-and-lasting-ideals/

Jackson, Nicholas. (2001). "Shark Week: Remembering Bruce, the Mechanical Shark in Jaws." *The Atlantic.* (August 3). Online at https://www.theatlantic.com/technology/archive/2011/08/shark-week-rememberingbruce-the-mechanical-shark-in-jaws/243026/

Michaelson, Gerald and Steven Michaelson. (2003). *Sun Tzu for Success: How to Use the Art of War to Master Challenges and Accomplish the Important Goals in Your Life.* Adams Media.

Peterman, John. (2000). *Peterman Rides Again: Adventures Continue with the Real "J. Peterman" Through Life & the Catalog Business.* Prentice Hall Press.

Prewitt, Edward. (1998). "Pitfalls in Meetings and How to Avoid Them." *Harvard Business Review.* (June). Vol. 3, no. 6.